AF454254

all about

NUMEROLOGY

Numbers rule our lives!

all about
NUMEROLOGY

Numbers rule our lives!

-By Renukka Sawhneyy Masst

KNOWLEDGE WORLD

KW Publishers Pvt Ltd
New Delhi

ISBN   978-93-94915-51-0   Hardback

Published in India by Kalpana Shukla

KW Publishers Pvt Ltd
4676/21, First Floor, Ansari Road
Daryaganj, New Delhi 110002
Phone: +91 11 43528107
Marketing: kw@kwpub.in
Editorial: production@kwpub.in
Website: www.kwpub.in

I am deeply grateful to the Almighty for choosing me as one of His favourites for helping Indian women especially, through the medium of numerology, psychology, counselling. There has been a long list of NRI's from Australia in particular, who have showered me with immense affection and gratitude as a reward for my services. Without exaggeration, I can say that my ocean of love for the infinite Supernatural Power is absolutely unquestionable.

Contents

Preface

The year 2001 carries immense significance for me as a human-being, as an Asian woman, as a mother of three children. In fact, I suddenly started growing up from a young plant into a full-grown tree. Earlier, my married life had been that of a hyper-active, over-concerned mother, and overly-occupied house wife, I found very little time to develop any talent or even to understand what my purpose in life was.

The miraculous twist in life happened when my maternal aunt visited me. She gifted me a book on Feng Shui, which is a beautiful science related to the correct placement of objects in the house. Being an English Hons. student from the University of Delhi, I have always been an avid reader.

My interest in reading the book on Feng Shui, led to my interest in improving the positivity, progress and achievements of not only my children, but also myself in life. The next additional venture was the study of Vastu and Tarot Card Reading. Finally it was Numerology which I became totally hooked onto. From being an Arts student, it took me several months, however, to switch over to Mathematics and calculations as a part of my daily routine.

From 2001, there was no looking back. With each passing day, while my children were clearing their ICSE and ISC boards, I too was practising how to work on birth charts of several family members and friends. With deep gratitude to Hans Decoz and Tom Monte, I studied and succeeded in mastering to a great extent the system of Pythagorean numerology.

Alongwith the research work of numerology as a mathematical science, I also did an analysis on the conversion of alphabets into numbers. This alphanumeric transformation helped me to comprehend the role of the name, in one's lifetime, which every individual is using ever since the time of birth. By adding up all the digits related to the nick-name, main name, surname, I experimented the usage of additional letters in the Name of a person. This method of changing the native's Name spelling, proved to be highly beneficial. People achieved multiple results as well as success in the fields of education, career, finance, travel opportunities, and family life. This is what I had been striving for. I did not wish to be a simple numerologist who can merely make conclusions on the past, present and future of anyone's life.

There needed to be some sort of good remedies that could help in the total improvement of an individual's life. In order to attain this positive outcome, the first technique I adhered to was the alteration of the spelling of a Name. The second and highly challenging methodology was the inclusion of religious items in the home and office area.

These were, mantras written out on boards, tarot charms, shells, metallic statuettes of Hindu gods and other similar solutions. I started out with Feng Shui objects such as: turtle, wind-chime, frog, dragon, and other similar items. However, I followed and practised this Chinese science only for a couple of years since these articles needed to be placed strictly in either North, South, East and West direction. My clients would invariably mess with these placements and I would be constantly reminding them of the right positioning of these pieces.

At the onset of this numerological journey, I would like to mention that by no means did I imagine that I was on the way to be an expounder of Numerology. My primary aim was to bring improvement in my own life and in my family. However after practising Indian Vastu, Chinese Feng Shui, Pythagorean Numerology, and doing Tarot Card reading between the years 2001 and 2005, I began to receive a favourable feed-back from my clients.

Of course I must admit that my family and friends encouraged and supported me to adopt this science as a profession. This was another milestone to my journey in Arithmancy which was a pre-20th century term for numerology. Henceforth, my domain for reaching out to clients became wide, business-like and professional.

Needless to say, it was a tough decision to step out into the market and to safeguard myself from making any mistakes while practising. My reputation as a diligent worker, and as a numerologist who could propel a person's life in a positive direction, is what I hankered for right from the start. We're now living in 2023 and for sure, till date, no one can doubt or be critical about my knowledge, dealing or remedial measures. I'm being specific about those whom I have worked for and not people who are disbelievers of this great practical science.

So, here I am, after studying the two main areas of Numerology, i.e. Horoscopic calculations and Name

Changing, my deepest desire and aim is to unfurl the flag of happiness, attainment of freedom from misery, and ill-health. Pythagoras (570-490 BC), the Greek philosopher and mathematician, has made an invaluable contribution to the world at large. In a nutshell, one can say that although every life on earth is born with a birth chart and destiny, yet there is immense scope of escape from the troubles which are supposedly pre-destined.

It can be explained easily by comparing two situations, one is that of a believer of numerology, and the other is that of a disbeliever. If both the characters are driving a vehicle towards a dark T point, the follower of numerological solutions will certainly take the left or right turn at the right time and thereby drive to a safe point. On the contrary, the skeptic can risk his safety by hitting the invisible and dark T point.

So who doesn't wish to escape harm and danger. Experience advocates the imbibing of solutions as heavenly medicines for horoscopic ailments. Through

22 years of practicing Numerology, I have discovered my aim in life, that is of helping myself and my fellow-women. This passion has been gradually increasing over the years and now I'm praying and hoping that people will benefit from my written experiences.

Renukka Sawhneyy Masst

About the Author

My journey in life has been very privileged and interesting. Having completed my schooling from St. Mary's Convent, Nainital, I had the opportunity to study English Literature from Delhi University. Although, I aspired to be a lecturer, I branched out to my second love, i.e. of being a social worker at the Missionaries of Charity, Civil Lines, Delhi.

Having done charitable work for a couple of years after college, I married, settled down, and now have a family of three beautiful children. Once they finished with their schooling I explored the field of Feng Shui, Vastu, Tarot Card Reading, with the aim of having an improved life. Once my skills were sharpened in these fields, I ventured into the field of Numerology.

Since then, there was no looking back. It was 2001 then and it is 2023 now. There has been an upward gradient in terms of success and professional achievements in India and overseas. Moreover, to add another feather to my cap I have been a member of an NGO since the past four years. It functions under the name of New Women Empowerment Team of Social Workers, Patiala, Punjab.

The main focus of my life is to help women of every class,community to develop their vocational skills and thereby become self-reliant. In order for these under-privileged women to achieve self-sufficiency, it is a sincere effort on my part to provide financial support to them so that their families are taken care of by way of food, education, development of talents, and provision of jobs as well.

The Almighty has given us one life.

Let us lead it with dignity and help others to do the same!

Renukka Sawhneyy Masst

Numerologist

Tarot Card Reader

Feng Shui & Vastu Consultant

Social Worker

https//:renumerology.com

Introduction

Numerology is a vast subject just as mathematics is. In fact it would be suitable to say that numerology is **Heavenly Mathematics**. God Almighty created the universe and mankind to inhabit the world and live a span going up to 100 years in rare cases though.

In order to rule the world in a fairly systematic fashion, he evolved a science called numerology. There are four well known methods of numerology. They are called **Vedic**, **Chaldean**, **Chinese** and **Kabbalah**.

PYTHAGOREAN NUMEROLOGY

There is a fifth process of studying numerology. It is also referred to as being 'Modern' and it focuses on six major numbers. Three of these are taken from the individual's date of birth. These are connected to the

Month number, **Day of Birth** number and **Destiny** number. The other three are taken from the name i.e. the **Expression** number, **Personality** number and the **Soul Urge** number.

Collectively speaking, these six numbers reflect upon the person's life in the internal and external sense. By studying these six numbers, valuable suggestions can be given to the native. The positive points can be highlighted and solutions be provided for the purpose of avoiding the impact of negative numbers and their malefic consequences.

There are various theories regarding the proclamation of the oldest method of numerology. There is no confirmation regarding this mystery. However one thing is certain, this science has great depth and it works too.

But then there is a common valid question cropping up in the minds of people who come to us as clients suffering from numerical difficulties and confusions. On the one hand they are desperately seeking solutions and on the other hand they are not sure whether these remedies work.

REMEDIES

Well, yes, these remedies do work. Although one has to accept the fact that destiny is pre-written yet God has created methods by which we can improve our lives. It's like saying that an alert sailor of a sailing ship can steer away his ship from a tumultuous storm while a laid back sailor of another ship may become a victim and cause others to become victims to the forthcoming storm. The job of a numerologist is to help the other person, rather people at large to change their direction to a safer shore.

Whether it is the sphere of education of children, one's own career, finance, relationship or marriage, every problem has a steering wheel which can be used to move away from the impact of an obstacle. Therefore brakes can be applied to the victim's suffering.